THE SPIRITUAL AMERICAN SERIES

MEDITATE FOR EVERYONE

Activating Your Benevolent Nature

Dr. Anne O'Hare

Printed in the United States of America

Library of Congress Control Number: 2026942003

Digital ISBN 979-8-234-08339-5
Paperback ISBN 979-8-9922520-2-6
Hardcover ISBN 979-8-9922520-6-4

Published by Alembic Press
Hotchkiss, Colorado

To every soul who wishes to help and support the world, who has faith in the connection between self-transformation and world transformation. This is the time of the greatest need, when the most elevated self-respect and world service are possible.

Contents

Foreword

I'M A SEEKER BY nature. Though where some seekers are pulled toward the metaphysical questions of why we're here or what happens when we die, my question has always been more practical: *how do we live well while we're here?* It's the question that has drawn me to spend more than twenty years studying philosophy across a wide assortment of contemplative and mystic traditions, including the theology of Christianity and other major world religions.

What I've grown skeptical of is what passes for "spirituality" in the current cultural moment—the influencer-friendly version that has hollowed out the word until it means little more than self-optimization with better lighting. Manifestation, alignment, abundance, your sovereign self: an entire vocabulary that turns the inner life into a vehicle for getting what you want. It is everywhere, and it is mostly empty.

So when I took on the work of editing this series, I wasn't guarded per se; I just didn't expect much. I learned quickly just how wrong I was. Anne is a serious practitioner of a tradition called Raja Yoga, taught by the Brahma Kumaris. This is a school of thought I'd never encountered before this project, and one that turns out to have remarkable depth and internal coherence. As a teacher, Anne didn't ask me to take her word for anything. She invited me to investigate, to just try it and see. She didn't make me wrong for needing intellectual understanding to precede emotional experience.

What I didn't expect when we started was how editing these books would change me.

In *Meditate Anyway* I learned that *I am a soul, and my nature is peace.* A simple truth that, in itself, feels like a memory of something I once knew, something I've been trying to get back to for most of my life. I was reintroduced to basic principles of spirituality we've all heard before: karma, personal responsibility, higher self. And yet…in modern interpretations of what is called spirituality, these principles often feel watered down. Anne gave them back their meaning, their substance, the weight that makes them worthwhile. I walked away from that book hopeful, beginning to feel an internal shift, and craving m ore.

Then we started *Meditate For You.* Anne wasn't joking when she told me this book would require something of me. It was an excavation—a slow process of distinguishing myself from the patterns I had mistaken for my*self.* I saw things about myself I can't unsee, patterns it would be easier to leave alone and pretend were caused by someone else. I struggled with being merciful with myself, and I resisted the whole not-forcing thing. (Because I am really good at forcing, at making things happen.) But I was compelled by the promise of freedom and by a distinct shift I kept noticing in my engagement with the world. I was becoming more of the woman I always wanted to be—the woman I felt certain was in here somewhere, if only the world would leave me alone long enough for her to emerge. It turns out the freedom comes from realizing I didn't need the world to go away for that to happen.

Then came this book, *Meditate For Everyone*. It is different, and it's the one I think I needed most.

This book reveals what the work is *for*. The work of this knowledge, the work of our lives, is to strip away what is not our nature so our true nature can emerge as benevolence. And the natural outgrowth of experiencing benevolence is service. Not service as obligation or as a virtue signal. Service as the inevitable shape of a self that has stopped blocking what it already is. You become someone who can actually give, and then giving becomes what you are.

I have always maintained the conviction that being human is for *something*—that the point is not pleasure, not comfort, not the cultivation of an interesting inner life for its own sake, but what we are willing to put back into the world. What this book gave me was language for something I had believed for a long time without being able to articulate it: the work on the self and the giving back are not two separate things. They are the same thing.

If you're like me, by the time you are reading this, you've put in the work. You can sense that something powerful, something essential, is within reach, but you can't quite see it yet. What you will experience as you move through the melding of heart and mind, of experience and intellect as Anne presents it here, is a delicate lifting of that veil of separation.

This book closes out the series, but the work it points toward doesn't end. This is the work of a lifetime, and you'll find yourself coming back here, cycling through, deepening, returning. Or at least, I know that is true for me, and I hope it is true for you too.

— Michelle Fishering
Editor of *The Spiritual American Series*

Introduction

MOST OF US KNOW what it's like when something arrives at the right time.

A book finds you the week you needed it. A friend calls just as you were thinking of them. Or you sit down to a conversation that, somehow, you were finally ready to have. We don't always have words for what's happening in those moments. We just recognize them. Some people call this divine timing. Whatever you call it, you've felt it—and you know that when you let the right thing arrive on its own schedule, instead of forcing it or pushing it away, life seems to cooperate with you in a way it doesn't otherwise.

I want to suggest that this same principle is at work on a much larger scale.

There is a time for human beings to wake up. To remember who and what we actually are. To turn toward the soul, toward God, toward each other, and to become useful to the world in a way we couldn't be before. That time is now.

I don't say this lightly, and I don't say it to alarm you: the world you are living in is not the same world it was even a generation ago. Things that felt stable are no longer stable. Institutions, assumptions, identities, ways of life—it is all shifting. You have noticed. Everyone has noticed, whether they admit it or not.

What is less obvious, but just as true, is that something else is moving with it. Spiritual knowledge that was once hidden, scattered, or available only to a few is becoming available now in a way it has not been before.

This is why I cannot practice spirituality independently of world events. I am part of this world. What is stirring in the world is also stirring in me, and what is stirring in me has somewhere it needs to go. In this time of upheaval, the world is full of fear and confusion, but through my individual spiritual practice, I can be an instrument for peace, hope, and healing in the world.

Don't be disheartened. Just as we have experienced freedom and peace in ourselves as a result of imbibing and applying this knowledge, so too will the world begin to be impacted. We have a tendency to focus on the sanskars we want to transform. But remember that we are emerging other sanskars: Peace, Love, Generosity, Brotherhood, Harmony with Nature. These energies are doing something. That is a law: first consciousness, then reflection in the world of time, space, and matter. Just saying that it is also time to allow our hearts to connect and hope for a wonderful future for ourselves and the world.

We will take this one step at a time.

Setting the Stage

In book one, *Meditate Anyway*, we discovered the essence of our spiritual identity: I am a soul, and my nature is peace.

And we also learned about spiritual laws such as the Law of Karma. This knowledge forms the foundation of the journey of self-realization. In book two, *Meditate for You*, we courageously did a deep dive into our sanskars, shedding light into the dark, and loosening the grip of sorrow-producing beliefs and habits.

In this book, the invitation is to completely release the old ways of functioning. To adopt a universal and benevolent context that naturally serves my self, all souls, and nature. As you begin reading this book, my suggestion is to take your time. With each new idea, give yourself time to digest, even on an emotional level. The aim is real transformation, which means allowing time for processing feelings and emotions. The ideas presented may bring reactions inside, questions. Just remain calm and patient and let your inner wisdom have a chance to e merge.

Renunciation of Old Patterns: A Disclaimer

You may be challenged by some of the ideas in this book. They are confronting powerful beliefs. If, at any time, it feels like too much, feel free to stop reading or even dismiss this book entirely. Nothing is being forced here. Also, there are times when we have such intense emotional pain in an area that we need to use therapy or other resources first and then return to this approach. This is about taking care of yourself where you are.

Study Plan and Resources

Hopefully, you have created a study rhythm while reading the first two books. Continue to give yourself a chance to absorb and digest the information. I invite you to locate on YouTube *The Spiritual American Podcast Channel, Guided Meditation Playlist, and Meditate for Everyone-Book Resources Playlist.* In several of the chapters, I will refer you to one or more of these resources or videos for practice.

Podcast Channel

Guided Meditations

Book Resources

A Blessing for You

This Spiritual American series is meant to be a blueprint for using Raja Yoga Meditation and Study to achieve Spiritual attainment. I am not a guru, nor do I profess to own the Truth. We are all souls, children of the Supreme Soul, and also conscient beings on this planet. We have the ability to be the masters of our minds and create our reality. Each of us has inner wisdom and power. My hope is that hearing this from someone with similar sanskars and who understands where we are coming from allows each soul reading this to easily imbibe what is being offered. Lots of love and heartfelt good wishes to each and every one of you on your own unique journey.

Let's begin.

Creating a New Context

Radical Self-Acceptance

Once you leave the cage, fly away free, forever.

S INCE BOOK ONE, WE have been practicing Merciful Self-Observation. We have been practicing soul-conscious awareness and observing the mind, observing my attitudes, my feelings, and my behaviors. I'm sure you all have had powerful insights and been able to transform behaviors through your efforts so far.

In this chapter, we will be going to the next level of freedom: Radical Self-Acceptance. Wow. Have we ever thought that self-acceptance would give access to freedom? In order to practice this, we need to become aware of a specific phenomenon that might feel so natural that we do not even notice it. I am talking about resisting and judging yourself, your feelings, your needs, and your natural inclinations. This resistance creates a "fight" in the mind, a sense of discomfort, a feeling of being trapped, and a compulsion to change what we think, feel, or spontaneously experience.

For example, I might be doing an activity, and internally, I may be disturbed by thoughts like "You should be doing something else, something more productive," or " You have been sitting too long, you need to exercise." Have you ever felt hungry at 9pm and had a war inside about whether to eat because it is "too late" and I "will gain weight"? Or even an inner argument about whether or not to say something. When this type of inner conflict is happening, I do not feel peace, happiness, or well-being. I would even go so far as to say that this experience is a clear obstacle to productivity as well. Struggling to accomplish tasks is not a recipe for peace and self-confidence.

To overcome this, the invitation is twofold.

First, practice merciful self-observation and see if you notice this type of resistance to your own natural living experience. Pay attention to your subtle feelings and thoughts while you are going about your day. See if you experience this type of self-judgment and critique of your thoughts, feelings, and actions in the moment. Just observe and validate that this is happening. It might also be helpful to notice where this inner phenomena originated. For instance, I grew up in a home where there was fighting and yelling all the time. It's natural that I would have internalized some of that environment.

Next, practice radical self-acceptance. Give yourself a chance to "just do" what you are doing and be ok, or don't do something and be ok. There has to be an action after the acceptance. We want to reinforce that it is possible to live without the inner war against myself.

Once you free yourself from this internal resistance, I invite you to never go back.

I have to say that this is *not* an invitation to indulge in addictions, extreme, or harmful behaviors. The presumption is that if you are reading this book, you are operating within a reasonable realm of functionality and behavior. This is about the possibility of permanently disabling the self-censoring sanskar. To experience freedom in the simple activities of living. To act based on your real, honest, and spontaneous feelings and desires.

It will take a while for the inner resistance, the arguments, and the disturbances to calm down. But the ride is a nice one. Every time you choose to act naturally, based on your authentic thoughts and feelings, in the moment, something deep and sweet gets validated. Your natural happiness, just being alive. This is our birthright as human beings.

Points for Contemplation and Practice

- Three times today, practice radical self-acceptance. Give yourself permission to experience this freedom in action. See how you feel and what happens in the circumstances.

Releasing Right and Wrong

When you let everyone play their part, you are finally free to play yours.

THE QUESTION OF WHO'S right and who's wrong feels like it's everywhere—in families, in politics, in the daily noise of just being alive in the world. Most of us were raised with a clear framework for this. Families, religion, and culture all provide clear, definitive buckets for judging others. But as you move through the process of remembering who you are under and apart from the sanskars, those frameworks begin to feel a lot less like solid ground and more like quicksand. *This is right, and that is wrong* becomes *I think this is right and that is wrong*—but wait, do I? And does it even matter?

Let's try on the idea that "right and wrong" may be a logical context; however, it is not bringing me happiness, peace, or harmony in my life. But what do you replace "right and wrong" with? How do you interact with the world, specifically the other humans who make up the world, without those scales of reference?

There are three laws we've talked about before that can help us create a new inner stage, a new point of view, a new attitude toward myself and the world. Let's look at these laws here individually.

The first is this: everyone is a soul, playing their own exact part.

Every single person you know, every person you'll never meet, every person whose choices baffle or hurt or infuriate you—they are a soul, moving through their own journey, playing a part that is uniquely and precisely theirs. Not the part you'd choose for them if you were in charge. Theirs. And here's what's interesting: even if you were given the chance to swap, you wouldn't actually want to. Their problems, their karma, their particular path, it belongs to them in a way that's oddly complete. You have your own part, and they have theirs. What this means practically is that the compulsion to correct people—to make them understand, to fix what they're doing, to hold them up against your standard of what's right—starts to lose its grip. Letting them play their part is a form of deep respect.

There is also a subtle aspect to this. You can apply this law to your own sanskars. You can use this law in your internal world. This is advanced practice that I invite you all to explore if you are so inclined. You need to have some level of emotional mastery to do it. But being stable and detached from your own mind, intellect, and sanskars brings a new level of experience, self-respect, and a feeling of spiritual progress.

The second law is harder for most of us to really absorb, even though we've heard it before: you are not responsible for anyone else's inner state, and no one is responsible for yours.

Now, if you have children, obviously, there are responsibilities. In marriage, in close relationships, there are real obligations. That's not what this is about. This is about the other thing we do, the thing that runs so automatically we barely notice it: making other people responsible for how we feel. *You hurt my feelings. You're disturbing me. If you would just behave differently, I could be okay.* We've all done it. Most of us still do it more than we'd like to admit. And on the other side, we spend enormous energy trying to manage what other people feel about us, adjusting ourselves constantly to keep the emotional weather around us stable.

That's a full-time job. And it's not actually your job.

When you really take this in, and I mean *take it in*, not just agree with it intellectually, it creates real freedom. Suddenly, there's much less to be angry about, much less to defend. If nobody is responsible for making me happy, then nobody can really take my happiness away either. That's a trade worth considering.

And then there's Karma, which is the third law and, honestly, the one that changes everything if you let it.

Remember, Karma isn't about punishment. It's not the universe keeping a scoreboard. It's more like physics—like the way throwing a ball at a wall means a ball comes back at you. Whatever energy you put out, in your thoughts, your feelings, your actions, the quality of that energy returns to you, not necessarily from the same person or in the same form. But t he *feeling* of it comes back. The generosity you give creates the conditions for generosity to find you. The indifference you operate from creates the conditions for indifference to greet you. It's not personal. It's just how it works.

The good news, and this really is good news, is that it means you are sovereign. Your inner life is your actual jurisdiction. What you cultivate in here is what you're planting out there. Which brings us to why any of this matters.

If you get pulled into the argument about who's right and who's wrong, if you let the world's noise get inside you and run your reactions, you become less useful to everyone, including yourself. The reactivity takes over. The judgment takes over. And you lose the one thing you actually have to offer: your own clarity, your own steadiness, your own genuine presence.

But if you can hold what's happening with understanding rather than verdict—*I see what's going on, I understand why people are the way they are, I don't have to fix it or adjudicate it*—you stay clean inside. And from that place, you can actually help by being a stabilizing presence, by giving what's actually needed rather than what the ego thinks is needed, by keeping your own energy clear so it doesn't add to the noise.

I need to be calm in order to help. Whatever you change inside yourself is making a difference for the people around you, for your relationships, for your body, for the atmosphere of every room you walk into. Purify your own inner weather. Let what naturally flows from that be your contribution. You don't have to decide who was right. You don't have to manage the score. You can watch all of it, all of the complexity and disagreement and human struggle, with compassion instead of judgment. And from that place, you are more present, more genuinely useful, more free.

One final thought and a gentle warning. You may be reading this, and after some contemplation, you may intellectually accept that it is possible to take on a perspective beyond right and wrong. Be ready then for pushback from your old sanskars. You will have to face all the areas where you have been rigid in your perspective. You will have to give up all righteousness, judgment, gossip, and complaining. You will have to learn to see things from the "opposite" point of view. You will even have to learn to honestly agree with your former "enemies". Be ready for this and face it with joy and understanding. The intellect opens the door, but the heart must pay the price for freedom. I am sure that you will do this and come out free and happy on the other si de.

Points for Contemplation and Practice:

- Notice any thoughts or questions that arise when considering adopting a perspective beyond right and wrong.

- Confirm within yourself how it feels to be soul-conscious. What feelings do I have for myself and others in this awareness?

- In what situations do you find it difficult to avoid judgment? Reflect on your own capacity for compassion and understanding.

- Journal on your ideas and insights.

Peace as a Lifestyle

Peace is not my aim; it is my inner vibration.

For a long time, I thought peace was something you arrived at. After the hard thing resolved, the relationship healed, or you finally got clear on the thing you'd been turning over for years. Then you'd be peaceful. It was always waiting on the other side of something.

Even in Meditation, the feeling is that I need to "calm down", I need to "heal", I need to learn concentration. We think meditation is a pathway to peace. Something I have to "do" to discover peace.

What's actually true is both simpler and closer than that.

Peace is your nature. It's what you are before all the accumulated noise, before everything you picked up along the way. The soul's nature is peace, the way water's nature is wet. That's not something water achieves; that's just what water is. Peace is like that. It's the fundamental nature of the soul. Not a state you work toward. Not a reward for getting it together. Just what you are, underneath all of it.

Which means the work we've been doing hasn't been about *building* peace. It is about uncovering it. Clearing out what was sitting on top of it. The peace itself was there the whole time.

If you have been practicing and self-reflecting since book one, my hope is that you have noticed subtle changes in your daily experience. Maybe you were surprisingly calm in a situation that you have reacted to in the past. Maybe you notice that you emerge empathy and understanding toward someone, where before there was judgment. Maybe you are more attracted to quiet and solitude, where before there was agitation. As we progress, we also start to notice more of our inner environment while performing daily activities.

For Instance, I'll be in the middle of something completely ordinary—cooking, driving, sitting at my desk—and I'll realize the noise is running. That low-level hum of urgency or friction or just vague dissatisfaction. Just observing this can be freeing, being the master of my inner world. But if I need to, I can quietly remind myself: *I am a soul. My nature is peace.* And then *feel* peace. I am gently creating my own inner experience based on the truth of who I am. Then, the noise settles. Dinner still needs to get made. I still need to cope with bad drivers on the road or get the work done. Whatever was on my mind might still be there, or not. But I've dropped back into what's actually true, and from there, everything is just...fine. I'm here. I'm doing this. All is well. That's peace, running quietly underneath whatever else is happening.

You can try it right now. Or today, sometime in a small moment like brushing your teeth, waiting in line at the coffee shop, or as you walk from one room to another. Let the awareness of peace be there. Look for it subtly, direct your attention toward the peace within. Then notice what happens, or more to the point, what doesn't happen. Nothing stops working. The ordinary thing continues. You just get to be present for it from a different place.

Remember to be patient and generous with yourself. Some moments may be too emotionally charged for you to fully access your own peace. That is ok. Observe everything with mercy, and remember that, in the observing, healing and transformation are activated naturally.

Points for Contemplation and Practice

- Reflect on the main principle of this chapter. That is, it is possible for me to experience peace while living every moment and doing every action. Ask yourself if this is theoretically possible.

- Take a few moments today during ordinary activities, and practice shifting your inner awareness to soul-consciousness and peace. Notice what happens inside you and in the physical scene.

- Journal on any new insights and experiences.

Pure Vision

*Pure vision means seeing through the eyes of
truth and feeling with the wisdom of the heart.*

YOU KNOW YOURSELF NOW. You've done the work of looking clearly at what you are and what you're not. This chapter is an invitation to look through that clarity—at the world, at the people in it, at the living world around you—and notice what you actually see. As you read the next several paragraphs, I invite you to open your experiential capacity, your creative mind, your "right brain," if you will. Let every word create an image, a connection, an understanding. We are now moving out of the realm of the ego-mind. Here we go.

Think of a time when time disappeared for you.

You were reading, or painting, or walking, or cooking, or absorbed in something that had no agenda, and when you looked up, an hour had passed. Maybe two. You weren't trying to be anywhere. You weren't performing, managing or explaining yourself. You were just there, moving through the thing, and time did what it always does when we stop watching it: it dissolved.

In those moments, something in you was free, open, present. The soul in its natural state doesn't experience time the way the rest of life does. It's the living part, the aware part, the one behind the eyes. And when it gets a little space, a little room to breathe inside the activity, it feels exactly like that. Like the hour that disappeared.

You've been here before. You're here now.

Imagine a point of light—the soul, your essential self—floating freely, not going anywhere in particular, not arriving anywhere, just moving through a nature scene, curious and quiet. And imagine that this little light comes to rest near a lake where an eagle is sitting in a tree.

What does the eagle know?

It's not thinking about itself. It has no concept of itself as "eagle"—no story, no history, no assessment of how it's doing. It's simply connected. To the water, to the sky, to the wind moving through the tree, to the pull of its own instincts, which are nothing more than nature moving through it. It acts from that connection without hesitation, without second-guessing, without psychological struggle. The eagle doesn't need to become anything. It already is what it is, fully.

There's something in you that recognizes this, that understands—just notice.

Now imagine that same little light moving toward a baby somewhere, just sensing its presence, just for a moment. What does it feel like to be near an infant?

So open. So sensitive to the slightest shift in energy. No armor, no history, no story about who's trustworthy and who isn't. Just a heart wide open to whatever is here.

That was you once. And more than you might think, that openness is still here; it didn't go anywhere. It's been underneath the whole time.

Now bring up an image of the people around you, in your life. Someone you know well, someone you have a whole history with, good or complicated or both. And for just a moment, imagine pulling away everything you know about them. The history, the friction, the role they play in your story. The name, the personality, the things they've said and done.

What's left?

A soul. A point of light. A living being, playing their part in this life, shaped by everything they've experienced, just like you. Trying, struggling, getting it right sometimes and not at other times, just like you.

Just like I have been, so are they.

That seeing is compassion. It doesn't mean everyone gets to do whatever they want to you. It doesn't mean collapsing into other people's pain. It means seeing clearly. And clear seeing, it turns out, is already a form of love.

Notice how it feels to look at someone that way, even for a few seconds. Notice how your inner vibration, your inner world, changes. How do you feel about yourself in that moment of truth, of clarity, of natural connection and positive regard?

This is what purity means. The essence of what you are, looking at the essence of what someone else is. Everything is fine just the way it is.

The floating soul moves gently through the world like this, sensing the harmony of the elements, the water and the sky, and the land, all doing what they do, none of it in conflict. There's a silence there. And that silence is in you, too, underneath everything.

You don't have to do anything with it. You don't have to manufacture it, or protect it, or announce it. When you look at the world from this place—even briefly, even imperfectly—you become, for that moment, a little window letting in the light.

Points for Contemplation and Practice

- Reflect on how it felt to see the world through the eyes of nature and of innocence.

- Journal your insights and experiences after the creative practice in this chapter.

How Blessings Work

*Blessings are our sweet invisible support
through life.*

I N MY AMERICAN UPBRINGING, as part of Western culture, the idea of blessings was limited to the church and priests. Whenever there was a "blessing" being given, it didn't feel personal or relatable to me. It felt like a ritual. In all my years practicing Raja Yoga Meditation with the Brahma Kumaris, I have come much closer to Indian Eastern culture, and I can tell you that blessings play a much larger role in practical life in those cultures. So, let's define blessings in three levels.

First, a blessing can be when you feel like you are getting something from someone else that you don't deserve. You don't feel any ownership of what is being given to you. This could also turn into a kind of dependency. In the East, there is a strong emphasis on being in the presence of someone holy or scholarly and receiving their blessing. People will spend hours and days waiting in line to see a holy person or to enter a holy temple. The belief is that they will get something automatically just from being with that person or devotional structure.

Second, a blessing can be when someone that you respect says something good about you, and even though you do not believe it now, because you respect the person, you accept it as your potential. This is the type of blessing I have seen a lot in the Brahma Kumaris culture. Blessing cards are routinely given at the end of meetings and gatherings. The cards represent a divine blessing just for you. In this environment, I would accept it as a blessing from "God" and try to feel the self-respect of that blessing. I love and respect God, so I try to experience what He says about me as true, as my potential.

The third level is deeper, more subtle, and has to do with service and the laws of Karma. If you give from a heart of service, you create a positive memory of yourself in others. When they remember you that way, you receive the blessing.

Here's the principle: when you give from a genuine heart, you leave a positive imprint on others. And when they remember you with love, that remembrance becomes sustenance for you. Blessings, at this level, are energy you created now returning to you.

This is where the idea of fortune comes in. At Levels 1 and 2, the blessing comes from outside—from a holy person, from God, from someone you respect. At Level 3, the blessing is actually the return of your own giving. Fortune is the word for what you've accumulated through that giving. It's your karmic inheritance; it belongs to you because you created it.

I remember one of our seniors in the Brahma Kumaris saying, "What is mine will not pass me." My scientific mind thought, "You still better plan. Do you have insurance?" But I was also touched by her faith. She trusted her own fortune. She knew that what she had given would return.

So, how do I tap into this energy of blessings, karma, and fortune? Understand that whatever energy I have, my thoughts, feelings, and generosity, can be used for service. I can serve with my mind. Every day, try your best to be quiet, humble, sweet, and generous as much as possible. Remember everyone with love, and one day you will feel that you are receiving the return of your own goodness, your own love, your own generosity of spirit. You can develop faith in this. Then blessings become your sweet support through life.

Points for Contemplation and Practice

- What is my current relationship to the words blessings, karma, and fortune?

- Ask yourself, am I ready to tap into my own subtle potential and experience the return of service?

- Whenever you remember, practice generating positive, loving feelings and good wishes for yourself, your body, all souls, and nature. Notice how you feel about yourself when giving in this way.

- Journal on your insights and experiences.

Breaking Through the Wall of Ignorance

Facing My Own Arrogance and Ignorance / Embracing Humility

One of the greatest things a person can do is admit when they are wrong without excuses.

Throughout my spiritual journey, it has always been important to me that everything is "real," "authentic," and "provable." People can say many things that sound good but then something may not feel completely right. Sometimes I am surprised by how seemingly skeptical I have been and how wary I am of believing in something that is false or lacks the recognizable weight of Truth. With this commitment to Truth, I had to become very adept and willing to look at my own shortcomings. This is not fun. Not all of spirituality feels comfortable. But if I want to be *really* free, I have to look at all of myself honestly and be willing to give up whatever is necessary to stop the negative karma.

So, what measure do I need to use to help me see what I need to see to be free?

Anything that causes sorrow for myself or others, even at the level of thoughts and attitude. In a word, we can call this sorrow-causing function *vice*.

For those of you with religious training, you will recognize this idea of not causing sorrow as being moral or just having a conscience. In order to operationalize these values, I am asserting here that we need to see and then overcome our vices, our violent sanskars. With this in mind, I will list some of the functioning vices that we need to actively and consistently recognize.

Consider each of these and how they may be operating in you.

- Being judgmental of self or others

- Self-abandoning, intolerant, dismissive

- Insensitivity to others' pain, even to the point of callousness

- Ignorance of the call for human respect and dignity for all

- Outright greed, choosing money over humanity

- Selfish immersion in my own plans and endeavors without consideration of how this affects others

When I start seeing these vices in myself and am able to overcome them in the moment, I open the door to a new experience, humility. Humility is when I can be with my own imperfection and the imperfection of others without judgment or violence. I see the vice, and I refuse to align with the hurtful energy. I will bow and give up anything to prevent hurting, to prevent the expression of vice into the world. This humble behavior is inspiring and healing for myself and others.

How do we notice these behaviors in ourselves? Look at the world. Every day, we are watching scenes unfold, and we are having feelings and reactions to what is happening. One way to be truly brave here is to use the external as a mirror for myself. For instance, if I am watching corruption and people suffering because of greed or indifference, I can ask myself, *When have I caused myself or others pain due to my own greed, selfishness, or indifference?*

This work is essential now. We need to get honest so we can restore our self-respect and spiritual power. The power that includes everyone and does not harm, ever.

So, what is the takeaway here?

Karma will balance whether we consciously change or not. And ignorance is not immunity from karma. That is the law. Wouldn't it be better to see the truth, admit it, and then really change? Wouldn't that make my life more valuable? Adopting this practice of seeing the truth about myself and others and then becoming non-violent in the moment is humility, is greatness. Remember that you will have to give something up: selfishness, greed, being right, making someone else wrong, being a victim, or holding on to old beliefs or attitudes. Is it worth it? You can practice and answer this for yourself. This courage and sacrifice are what is most needed in the world now.

Points for Contemplation and Practice

- Write down your initial thoughts after reading this chapter. Understanding that words are limited, take a moment to reflect on whatever point was meaningful to you.

- Invite yourself to commit to courage, honesty, and renunciation of vice and violence in your thoughts, attitudes, and actions.

- Consider that one step of courage in a new direction will invite new and powerful help.

Releasing Dependency / Emerging Royalty and Dignity

*Royalty and Dignity are our birthright and the
glory of humanity.*

W HEN WE ARE AT the *mercy* of any authority outside
ourselves, even with the best of intentions and
surrender in our hearts, there will inevitably be sorrow and
confusion. It is hard to even think of living in a world where
I am not following some set of imposed rules. In spirituality,
the aim is to leave sorrow behind and step into a natural living
experience, a life that naturally flows in harmony with others
and with nature, a life of royalty and dignity. But how do we
begin to access this experience?

Conscience is an idea that we keep on a shelf reserved for
when we do things *wrong*, when we need to make amends,

go to confession, repent, etc. But when we begin to look at royalty and dignity, we can start by seeing conscience as our spiritual guardrail. Conscience is that sinking feeling after an interaction with someone or an impactful life event. The deep feeling like something is wrong. What if we were to start seeing that feeling *only* as a signal that I need to emerge my own royalty and dignity?

We have been trained to use that signal of the heart to subjugate myself further, to confess, to feel guilty, to reach out to someone for forgiveness or absolution, to obsess over how bad I am for hurting someone, or for not taking care of myself based on externally imposed measures. If we look closely, we can see that our conscience is simply alerting us that something is happening inside that is causing me to hurt. I have moved away from my safe, stable, benevolent nature, and this feeling of pain is signaling me to get back on my inner throne.

Just in case you are wondering, this invitation to follow your own inner counsel is not permission to be disruptive in the world. On the contrary, when I am on my inner throne of royalty and dignity, I am naturally and happily cooperative with whatever customs and systems I am physically engaged in. But internally, I am completely free and self-sovereign.

So, what is the inner throne? Let's use the rest of this chapter to explore the experience of royalty and dignity within.

Royalty means that I know myself to be a unique and sovereign being. One who has everything I need from inside. This quality expresses itself as a slight sense of detachment from the world and others. Detachment only in the sense of distinction—*not separation*. We need to start getting this right. This idea of emotional merging as closeness, and being constantly dependent on others for one aspect of life or another is not necessary and is actually negative Karma. So, let's try this today. Walk around with the awareness that you are an individual sovereign being, and that everyone else is an individual sovereign being as well. See how that feels. That is the foundation of *respect*. Self-respect and respect for others. Also, there is no need to add any labels or further distinctions here. Being is enough.

Dignity means that I am maintaining my self-respect, no matter the circumstances. I am able to remain calm, unaffected, and uninfluenced by all things perceived, both internal and external. That can seem like a tall order, especially the way the world is at this time, where all things that were once experienced and stable and supportive are becoming corrupt and unreliable. However, this is the time when dignity matters most.

I believe it is natural for us to want and even expect things to work out, to feel good, to last. But if we are honest, we have very little control over our life circumstances. We will talk about that more in a later chapter. For now, let's consider the idea that I actually have the power and inner strength to maintain my self-respect, my dignity, in *all* circumstances. That includes situations ranging from the computer not working, to health of the body, painful interactions with others, loss of resources or human support, feelings of loneliness or fear, even the death of this physical body. It is possible for me to remain stable and internally proud through all of it.

I am a soul, a being of subtle light and peace. I exist beyond time and distinct from matter. And I have an unbreakable and imperishable source of life inside me. I am eternally connected to the Supreme Soul and to all souls. There is nothing to fear.

These thoughts of pure pride and dignity can be practiced in all situations. Try and see. You may be surprised to find out how truly powerful you are.

Points for Contemplation and Practice

- Note down your thoughts and feelings about being at the "mercy" of external rules. What has been your experience?

- Reread the definitions of royalty and dignity above. Practice for yourself and journal on your experiences. Reflect on what may be possible when I am able to remain on my inner throne.

Disabling Fear and Reactivity / Establishing Self-Trust and Self-Reliance

A flower cannot stand up to a bulldozer.

AS WE CONTINUE TO practice merciful self-observation, my hope is that you have made real progress in recognizing and taking responsibility for your thoughts, feelings, and actions. In my many years of practice, I have noticed that even though I am consistently and reliably doing the "right" thing in all situations, I am often plagued by an internal sense of unease, confusion, and fear.

My inner world has, over time, become like a raw nerve. Any sound, light, person, or feeling coming through the senses stimulates an overwhelming cascade of subtle memories, of hurt feelings, and the initiation of internal defense mechanisms. Some of these may include self-hating thoughts, overactive interest in others' thoughts and behaviors, emotional reactivity, neediness, etc. When this is happening, I am in a state of confusion and fear. I am not here, present with myself internally at this moment. I may be able to do the right thing externally due to years of outward training and the pressure of social norms. But internally, there is a tidal wave, a hurricane of emotional instability, fear, and confusion. Is there any wonder that there is so much mental illness in the world?

Here, psychology must be re-evaluated and seen as no longer useful. Consigning myself to a developmental context where I am always emotionally dependent on others, or chasing after the assigned developmental needs of the past, is making me crazy. Take a moment now to consider if what I just wrote has validity to you.

Looking back over my life, I can see how psychology has become the "religion" for understanding my inner world and feelings. It is a religion of dependency. When I look now from a spiritual standpoint, from a place where I genuinely and humbly wish to live without fear, I can see that this past religion has taught me to be helpless, excessively emotional, reactive, and basically a slave to outside stimuli, including other people. Look at how technology and media are stepping in to take advantage of this inner fear and dependency.

It's ok. This is all happening so we can become free.

So what can I do to help myself move away from the old conditioning that is now creating a tumultuous, completely unlivable inner world, and into freedom, peace, and a natural life as a pure human being? First, I invite you to read over the chapter again up to this point. Make some notes and take a moment to validate these ideas for yourself.

Now, here are two practices that will help us to move towards freedom, purity, self-trust, and self-reliance.

The first practice is about protection and emotional freedom. Pulling back until the fear stops. There will be a place where it will stop. Have faith in this. This is detaching from the senses. What do I mean by pull back? Become sensitive to when you are feeling unease or fear in your body. You may be surprised to find how much of our life is spent in this energetic state. Then, in the moment, while the fear is there, begin to withdraw your attention inward. Away from any external stimuli and then away from the feeling itself. Locate the still silence inside you and gently begin to pay some attention to that. Do not be forceful here. Be present to the fear and, at the same time, gently allow yourself to be aware of the silence that is also there. You are not abandoning your feelings; you are gently and silently shifting the flow of energy from emotional expression through the body toward stillness, silence, and peace. This is going to take practice. You may only get a few seconds of relief. But you are starting to move in a new direction internally where you are truly emotionally safe and secure.

Second, develop an alternative view of your participation in this world: I am an angel. My presence provided something in my household and to my family in every scene of my life. Look beyond psychological needs and judgments, beyond the idea of developmental limitations. Look at the pure interactions. For example, my mother was able to talk to me and confide in me. In psychology, I was a helpless child at the mercy of wounded and ineffective parents who failed to meet my needs. From this new place, my mother was in pain, and my presence provided comfort for her. Maybe my heart can rest there.

This may feel like a big stretch. But consider all the pain and suffering experienced in the context that others were "supposed" to give this to me. Or I was "supposed" to get that. I never did. So, what am I going to do? Keep suffering? Psychology does not have a satisfactory answer here; the old context of needing remains: more dependency, more suffering, and endless emotional justification and indulgence.

As we move into the next several chapters, we will be exploring life beyond fear. Natural, pure being in the world. Like a flower. In this analogy, the old inner world is like a bulldozer. The flower doesn't have a chance against that. So, can I let go of the other context? I have to. It's time to move beyond fear and confusion. Beyond hurt and poor self-confidence.

For this, I need to pull back until the fear stops. To see myself as an angel in my own life. To experience life beyond Psychology, the science of the psyche. To consider that it is now time to choose real life over science and religion. Time to be a flower.

Points for Contemplation and Practice

- This may be the most confrontational chapter in this book because it directly exposes our consciousness of emotional dependency. Read it again slowly. Let yourself entertain the idea that living without fear is possible. Be gentle and journal your thoughts and feelings.

Renouncing the Illusion of Control / Be a Child and a Master

Child and Master—the balance that sets us free.

W HAT WILL HAPPEN TO me as I continue to discern the vices (sorrow-producing attitudes, thoughts, and actions) in myself and renounce them?

Slowly, I will begin to become aware of a new feeling inside. A sweet, stable, and generous-hearted self-energy. It will be small at first, but it will be unmistakable and also recognizable as me. This is purity. The new self, which is also the original self.

In this chapter, we will look at the two sides of this new pure self energy: Child and Master.

Let's start with Child—the pure heart.

Some qualities of child consciousness would be purity, openness, emotional safety, cooperativeness, trust, spontaneity, caring, and innocence.

Take a moment and reflect on the ideas we have about children. In my experience, most of what we focus on today is children's vulnerability or maybe lack of power. When we go beyond these fear based aspects, we can appreciate the pure qualities of children. We can recognize purity and innocence as greatness.

Purity and innocence are also a protection. A child is not aware of worldly matters, and so they do not react as adults do. It is as if they are living in a different world. Children are honest, have open hearts, and are naturally cooperative. They approach everyone with a sweet, loving attitude. An open heart is a gift that brings happiness to everyone.

Then we come to Master—the loving intellect.

Qualities of master consciousness include loving discernment, authentic self-expression, creativity, and the ability to face life circumstances, maintain self-integrity, and safeguarding the feelings of others.

We are able to feel valuable and confident in the world. No longer hiding or censoring myself, but standing by myself and my contribution in the world.

I also have a deep sense of my own innate value, even without doing anything. I know that just my presence is a positive contribution.

So, how do we practice Child and Master, and begin balancing these energies?

Imagine that you are with your family planning a vacation, or in a church group discussing upcoming holiday celebrations, or in a board meeting at work. There will always be the opportunity to participate, to share your ideas. But then, it is a good idea to be cooperative, to give supportive energy to the group. We have a saying in the Brahma Kumaris, "Give your ideas like a Master, then cooperate like a Child." The essence of this practice is to learn how to live and participate in life naturally and safely. You are the master, giving your idea without ego or attachment, and then you are the child, immune to feelings of insult and naturally cooperative with whatever is happening.

As we practice this balance of child and master, the new balanced self can emerge. This is part of the process of healing the heart, restoring my self-respect, having the heart of service to all, and preparing for the future world.

As I am writing this, I need to address the elephant in the room. This overdeveloped consciousness of *doing* that I believe many of us have. It seems that no matter what is happening, I may have the impulse to judge, to analyze, to fix, to solve, to change. This forceful energy will block the energies of child and master.

This may be the hardest thing to accept: *We actually do not have control over circumstances.* We only have control over our inner world, and even that power, we have lost and have to work to regain. Consider that somewhere along the line we started choosing feelings of control over peace, over health, over love, over connection. I'm sorry, but we have to get through this. We have to take responsibility. I cannot be forceful and peaceful at the same time. I cannot be judgmental and loving at the same time. I cannot be generous if I am afraid. Let's just face this head-on. We sold out our hearts for control. Take a minute for this to land. It is ok. We are all in the same situation. Time to face it, heal, and move on.

In the next several chapters, we will explore the qualities of gentleness and natural living, with sensitivity that actually empowers us and makes us happy. It may just be everything you didn't know you needed.

Points for Contemplation and Practice

- Reflect on the two sides of the "new" self, the pure energy—Child and Master. Write down your initial thoughts and include how these ideas may be different from the way you have thought in the past.

- Gently observe yourself and notice the "elephant in the room" as described above. Resist the urge to judge yourself. Emerge humility and forgiveness for yourself. Understand that this is the human condition at this time. I am no better or worse than any other soul. I have to accept where I am in order to get better.

- Practice Child and Master energies today. See where you can project the purity of a child or the compassion and understanding of a master, then let go completely to whatever happens. Practice relying on your own intention and experience, and less on what happens next.

Personality of Purity

Wisdom of the Heart

Where the mind thinks, the heart knows.

OUR FIRST STEP INTO this new personality of purity is moving from the ego mind into the heart. It is not so easy to talk about this because it is the language of being and knowing. There is very little to distinguish. The heart knows things the mind cannot argue with. You have felt this, even if you have not called it by name. So, I will give a few examples and then leave you to your own observation and discovery.

Do you want it?

Think about a time when you have chosen a path in life or left a path in life simply because you wanted it or didn't want it. This cannot be argued with, and no one has the power to change your mind at this level. No matter what the circumstances, how difficult the road may be, or the logical justifications, once this wanting or not wanting is activated, nothing will stop the soul from changing and fulfilling.

For example, at one time, I was in a professional program moving towards a new degree. I was registered, committed on paper, and paid my money. While sitting in the first class, I *knew* this was not for me. I do not want this. So I quit, that day. That whole future disappeared from my life. I never had another thought about it.

Think about a time in your life when you just knew, "I want this" or "I don't want this," and then your life moved in that new direction. No logic can touch this place, this inner knowing of the heart.

Falling in love

We sometimes talk about falling in love as something that cannot be controlled, as if it were "happening" to us. If we look more closely, we will see that falling in love is a subtle choice and a surrender of the heart. I have chosen this other to mean everything to me. After this deep choice is made, so many of my thoughts, hopes, and dreams are then subtly shared with this other. There is a wish to be as close as possible so I can share my whole self. In spirituality, we can say that we are using this power in relation to myself, God, and the world.

Acceptance to the level of stillness

This may be likened to Kubler-Ross's fifth stage of grief—acceptance. There is no more thinking, no more emotional processing. I am at peace with the situation. The mind becomes silent, and there may even be a sense of sweet contentment. At this level, no one else is involved. You are by yourself, and you accept. Try to remember a time when you felt this way.

Choosing other over self

We have all had moments in our lives when we have sensed the needs or feelings of others, and we gently and silently adjusted ourselves so they can feel whole or satisfied. No one knows what I am doing inside but me. And I will never share this internal process with anyone. This is the sweetness of generosity, of selfless love. We are all capable of this; we can develop this power and sensitivity to others.

You may have other examples of heart wisdom in your life. This wisdom is so powerful, and yet we do not pay much attention to it. Maybe it is time for the heart to lead more often.

Points for Contemplation and Practice

- Write down your initial thoughts and feelings after reading this chapter. In what areas of your life can you say that your heart has led you? In what areas do you think would be improved if the heart were allowed to lead? Imagine one area of your life and write about what it would mean to lead from the heart.

Be a Flower

The purest self-respect is the sweetness of knowing your worth independent of everything else.

WHAT IS YOUR FAVORITE type of flower? Visualize that flower now. What feelings and thoughts arise? If I were to ask you why that is your favorite, what descriptive words would you use? Maybe we never thought this much about flowers before, but flowers play a unique part in our lives. They are given as gifts, as signs of affection, gratitude, celebration, or even for condolences. So what do flowers represent? In this chapter, we will look at the characteristics of flowers as the soul's qualities. When reading about these qualities, try to feel them in yourself and give them experiential validity.

Living in a state of non-initiation and gentleness

Imagine what life would be like if I never initiated anything again? What would happen? Would life even continue? Flowers don't *do* anything. Just consider that. They are there, giving fragrance, attracting others' attention, but they do not assert themselves. They are just there, being.

Now, you may be thinking, Well, we have to do things. We are talking, moving, and interacting. Yes, this is true. So, let's add gentleness to the mix. When I am in an interaction, I can be gentle. If I am offering something, let it be with humility and sensitivity to the feelings of others. I do not wish to disturb. That is gentleness. So we can practice non-initiation and gentleness as aspects of purity in life.

Tasting the sweetness of your own presence in the world

I had a teacher once who said, "You will never taste the sweetness of rice if you keep eating cake." We are generally very connected to our senses and engaging with whatever is happening around us. To taste the sweetness of my own presence, I have to practice holding my attention on how I feel about myself in the moment. As I make spiritual progress, I am beginning to feel better about myself. I have positive regard for myself. Consider that your existence brings beauty and joy to the world. This is pure pride. We see this naturally in children. For practice, try to generate this feeling of pure pride and the happiness of just being here.

No longer thinking about anyone, yet you feel connected to all

An interesting paradox happens when we start paying attention to ourselves in a pure way; we stop thinking about other people, yet we feel full and satisfied inside. This is a quiet, subtle experience, but very beautiful and powerful. Think about animals in nature. They are not thinking about what others said or did, and they are not worried about their next interaction. Animals live in the moment with natural dignity. They interact fully, and then also are themselves fully. Think about this. What thoughts or feelings arise in you with this idea of living in the world without thinking about anyone else?

The mind is empty and yet full of pure feelings about myself.

When emotions and thoughts recede, we become filled with pure feelings. We are so used to thinking and language that we may even be a little afraid to let go of those functions. The idea of being "lost" in feelings feels scary. Let's just introduce the idea that if 90% of language was gone, I would still be here, still be able to live, interact, and be happy with myself. We can use flowers, nature, and young children to give us a sense of this stage.

Human beings are the decoration of the natural world

Finally, let's consider that human beings are the highest functioning lifeforms on earth. We have an intellect that allows us to master ourselves and the matter that surrounds us. We are very special and powerful. Can I own this status with humility? Can I start seeing myself as a pure and powerful soul, capable of real love and benevolence? Little by little, I am moving my consciousness, my self-awareness, in this direction. What could possibly be a better use of my time?

Points for Contemplation and Practice

- Make a note of your favorite flower and the

characteristics that attract you. Consider that those qualities that you appreciate are in you. How does it feel to think of yourself like that?

- Practice non-initiation this week. Value your own presence in every scene of your day. Be gentle and sensitive in all your interactions. Try to keep paying attention to yourself, your own beauty. Journal on your experiences.

Relationship with Nature

We are stardust, we are golden...and we've got to
get ourselves back to the garden.
—Joni Mitchell

W E ALL HAVE UNIQUE thoughts and experiences with nature. The thought of nature brings up images, memories, and feelings in our minds. The soul, consciousness, is in relationship with, or you could say dancing the dance of life, with nature. In the personality of purity, the soul is actually a perfect match with nature. Let's explore some ideas and practices that will help us re-establish our soul-conscious relationship with nature.

What if all the ideas we have about romantic relationships with other human beings are really about I, the soul, and nature? What if nature is really my Soul Mate in this human life on Earth? Sit with this idea for a moment and write down your initial thoughts.

Many of us have ranked being in love among the top human experiences. That is the happiest time, when all limits are removed from my heart, and I feel totally seen, connected, and free. From the soul's perspective, nature provides all of those experiences. I can only express myself with the cooperation of matter, nature, with this body.

So, let's take a moment and ask ourselves: *how do I feel about nature?* Maybe I have never considered my body as part of nature before. But doesn't this body come from the earth? And when the body's timeline is over, doesn't it go back to the earth?

Stretch yourself here. Consider yourself to be a soul, a point of living light. You are using a body to play your part. How does it feel to have a body, to express myself? To have senses that can see, hear, and touch. How do I feel about the natural world around me and my body?

Now this is going to sound a little "out there", but I want you to write a letter to the Earth, to nature, to the elements. Write from the point of view of a soul. You can talk about your body and all the beauty and wonder of nature on Earth. Remember, we are part of nature, and the Earth takes care of us just as it does all other living things. You can think of a particular animal or nature scene that you like. Imagine that you are subtly having a conversation with nature.

Now, imagine what it would feel like to be in energetic harmony with nature, starting with my own body. Think about a nature scene that you enjoy. What feelings are you experiencing? Notice the quality of your thoughts and also how you feel about yourself. Do you feel separated, alone, fearful, or sad? Or do you feel something else? Something universal, harmonious, and peaceful?

Finally, imagine a world where everyone is soul-conscious and in perfect vibrational harmony with nature. Focus on the feelings, especially how you feel about yourself in that environment. What if life on Earth was like this at one time, and I am simply remembering?

My hope is that you take your time with the above ideas and practices. Give your mind and heart a chance to experience something new and also something profoundly essenceful. The pure relationship between consciousness and matter—nature.

Points for Contemplation and Practice:

- Read this chapter again slowly and journal your experiences. You may also wish to create using an artistic medium, such as music, poetry, painting, sculpting, or drawing. Enjoy and Play.

Pure Consciousness-Pure World

Happiness is our human inheritance.

W HAT IF I TOLD you that true happiness is just being happy to be alive? Do you remember this? We all have this happiness inside. We have not lost it. It is buried, like the princess and the pea. And if you remember the story, only a princess could sense the pea under the mattresses. All of us are princes and princesses. We all have the inheritance of happiness. And what are the qualities that make us royal, that make us able to experience this happiness? Purity and innocence.

Before we practice, I would like to acknowledge the way things are now to help the intellect and also to stimulate compassion for myself and everyone.

When walking outside, notice how animals run from humans. This is subtly painful, and I wish I could be close to the animals, hug them, and pet them in nature. Also, the fact that we have to deal with illness, money issues, violence, and sorrow in relationships doesn't feel right or natural to the heart. So, it is okay to wish for the world to right itself again. The wonderful and miraculous thing about consciousness is that we have the power to change our inner world back to purity, back to innocence, and yes, back to happiness. We then become beacons of these vibrations in the present world (service) and also become cooperative in the transformation of this world into the future world (Heaven on Earth).

Ok, so for those of you who are having feelings about the word Heaven. I simply mean purity, innocence, and a world where humans are soul-conscious and in perfect harmony with nature. We were that way once, and we are becoming that way again. It is helpful not to *believe* this outright, but simply try on the idea that consciousness comes before physical reality, like a blueprint comes before a building. Pure consciousness creates a pure world.

With all the work we have been doing here clearing away old, crusty, painful sanskars, how would it feel now to *just be happy?* Take a deep breath now. Feel the right pride in your efforts and transformation so far. Close your eyes, breathe, and say to yourself, *I am here and everything is good.*

Now let's practice. Here are some thoughts to point our heart and mind in the direction of purity, innocence, and happiness.

Watch how silent and serene animals are. Wouldn't it be wonderful if we could get close to them, communicate with them, and play with them? The memorial of this is in fairy tales, the enchanted forest. Animals and humans are playing, dancing, and communicating in happiness. These fairy tales are made for children, why? Children have just arrived; they are new and happy just being here. Do you remember when you just arrived? Do you remember what that felt like? Try to remember the feeling. Look at a tree, a duck, a squirrel or a human child. Feel the purity, the sweetness, the innocence, the dignity, and the joy.

Find this for yourself. Happiness is right next to you, all around you, inside you. Peace, Purity, Innocence, and Happiness. This is our birthright, our pure and elevated inheritance as human beings.

Points for Contemplation and Practice

- Give yourself the gift of thinking about our human inheritance. Write your ideas. Use art to express your feelings. Remember, consciousness comes first so you are free to create and fulfill your heart.

4

Spirituality: From Knowledge to Experience

Spiritual Aims

Time to make my spiritual aims spiritual.
Transformation requires power.

RETURNING NOW TO THE soul side of our spiritual efforts.

Most of us have aims. We want to finish school, build a career, and raise a family. We set goals and move toward them. But a spiritual aim? That phrase might not mean anything yet. Or it might sound like something reserved for monks and mystics, not for ordinary people living ordinary lives.

And yet, when I ask people what they're reaching for spiritually, they usually have an answer. "I want to calm my mind." "I want to be less reactive." "I'd like my relationships to work." These are real desires, but what they have in common is that they're all about improving personality and circumstances. Becoming a better version of who we already think we are.

That was me, before Raja Yoga. I wanted to fix myself. I wanted to stop being confused. I wanted to improve. And I figured that if I did what I was supposed to do, God would basically give me what I wanted. That wasn't entirely wrong—I still believe there's a relationship between pure desires and karma, between facing what's in front of you and opening space for what you want to come. But the point here is to see what becomes possible when we stop using spirituality to fix ourselves or our circumstances and instead allow our spiritual aim to actually be spiritual.

Let me explain.

The main principle of Raja Yoga meditation is that I am a soul and my nature is peace. My nature is love. My nature is benevolence. This isn't something I need to achieve; it's something I already am. So the first spiritual aim becomes simple: I would like to feel more of my original nature. That's what meditation is for. I sit still, and I tell myself, *I'm a soul. My nature is peace.* And I try to feel that peace—not as something given to me by a person or a situation, but as something that belongs to me. Something that is me.

Then comes the second aim, which arrives when you're introduced to the Supreme Soul, to God. In this understanding, I am a soul, and God is also a soul. I am a living point of consciousness, and God is also a point of living consciousness.

When I first heard that God is a point and I am a point, that He's not bigger or smaller than me, something in me relaxed. I felt happy. I could tune into God's frequency—stillness, peace, purity, benevolence—and connect at a vibrational level. Soul to soul. Energy to energy. And so another aim became clear: I want to increase my connection with God.

God is the Ocean of Peace, the Ocean of Love. Unlimited. Surrendered for service. God doesn't take anything, not even a body. He's benevolent, wise, full of knowledge and peace. And that's my Father. So the aim deepens: I want to be like God. And I sense that at the spiritual level, I already am the same. I'm already like God in terms of qualities. What I'm growing is my capacity to live from those qualities—and to serve from that place.

A third aim has to do with how I move through the world. Living harmoniously without violence or force, navigating relationships and days without causing sorrow, without taking sorrow, without feeling disturbed. There can be a lot of noise in the mind, and none of us gets to skip that. We're all finding our way back to our original nature. But as that noise settles, I'm no longer forcing calm onto the surface while turmoil churns underneath. The disturbance actually dissolves. In the middle of my day, I find myself thinking: *I exist. I'm here. I'm alive. And everything's okay.*

Is it possible to live without all that noise? Without the jealousy, the anger, the upset?

Look at nature. The birds aren't jealous. The tree doesn't complain about the clouds. There's no grievance, no resentment, no self-criticism. I'm not talking about survival instincts—those are different. I'm talking about the emotional static we carry, the suffering we add. I don't need the jealousy. I don't need to feel bad about myself. None of it is necessary. It can fall away. And when it does, I become like the flower blooming, just being what I am.

So these are spiritual aims. These are aims that are beyond the ordinary. Do you have a spiritual aim? Would you like to have one? When we have an aim, our life becomes powerful and meaningful.

Points for Contemplation and Practice

- What is a true spiritual aim?

- Have I accepted the foundation of soul identity and experience of my nature as a soul?

- What is my relationship with God, the Supreme Soul?

- Based on the discussion above, what are my spiritual aims?

- Spiritual aims discussed in this chapter:

  - To feel more of my original nature as a soul

  - To increase my connection with God and to become more like God

  - To live harmoniously as a human being

God, Consciousness, and Raja Yoga Meditation

*Truth can be received through the intellect
or the heart.*

WHY DO WE DO meditation? Ask yourself this question now. Why am I practicing meditation? In the last chapter, we explored the idea of spiritual aims and learned that one possible aim of meditation is to have "spiritual" experiences. In this chapter, we will review receiving spirituality through the heart and spirituality through the intellect. Raja Yoga offers access to both. And both are needed for real transformation. So, let's explore the three principles that we need to understand as our knowledge base for practice.

First is the Soul, the Self. We have accepted and practiced this main principle since Book One. I am a Soul, and my Nature is Peace. This is a new identity and also a recognition of my forever identity. This is the first lesson of spiritual knowledge.

Second is God. Generally, and I would say logically, any spiritual conversation leads us to the subject of God. In Raja Yoga understanding, God is the Supreme Soul, a point of light. And also the "Ocean" of all the soul's natural qualities: Love, Peace, Purity, Power, Benevolence, Wisdom. In meditation, we are relating to God Soul to Soul. We relate to God in our mind, alone—a pure, incorporeal experience, connection, and realization. In Raja Yoga, the Soul and God are equally important, like a parent and child. Each sees itself in the other, naturally connected, naturally loving.

Some of us are still not fully comfortable with the subject of God. We strive to regain our own power and understanding. For this, we move to the third principle, the science of consciousness. When we study the spiritual knowledge shared in these books, we begin to see everything from an elevated point of view. We understand the relationship between consciousness and matter, being master of the mind, regaining emotional sovereignty, and the deep laws and philosophy of Karma. When we come to spirituality through the intellect in this way, we literally reason our way out of sorrow and confusion and into peace and alignment with natural laws.

I would argue that every one of us naturally leans toward either the devotional (God) or the intellectual (Study and Understanding) approach. This is fine, go with whichever feels natural to you.

In the opening of this chapter, I said that both approaches are needed for real transformation. So, let me make that case by telling a short story. I was watching a guru one day online. One that I like, who talks a lot about consciousness and detaching from the mind. One of the students asked, "Then who do I pray to?" This was very touching. It was a question from someone who favored the devotional approach but was willing to accept all the science of consciousness (as evidenced by his presence in that gathering). It was definitely a moment. The guru smiled and explained that consciousness allows for you to relate Soul to Soul with God and feel that love, companionship, support, and connection. We can also stand alone, independent, in perfect self-awareness and bliss. *Both* are available, and we have access to both. What a wonderful answer.

Studying and building your independence and self-respect does not take away your love for God or your ability to be sweet and humble, with a heart for service.

Inversely, opening my heart to know, love, and appreciate God as my beloved Parent, Teacher, and Guide, as the source of all virtues, powers, and knowledge, does *not* take away my ability to be independent and to self-realize with honesty and dignity.

It is possible to make spiritual effort without bringing God in as a separate being. On the consciousness side, as we understand more and more, we automatically become calmer, softer, less reactive, and more compassionate. But I think we also need belonging and the possibility of safe relationship. I am free and safe on my own, and I am free and safe in relationship with God.

This is a balanced approach. And it is accurate and sensible to be able to master both sides.

This is Raja Yoga.

We are working on both sides of the equation. This conversation is not about "religion". The ideas here are not in conflict with any culture or religious belief system. It's about gently identifying which side of this learning and receptivity equation you naturally land and then work with your strength and nurture the other side.

Points for Contemplation and Practice

- Which side of the spirituality equation do you naturally land on? Devotional or Intellectual? Surrender or Independence?

- Reflect on the three principles explored in this chapter: Soul, God, and the Science of consciousness. Think about what each one means and write down your own definitions.

- Access the Book Resources and contemplate the image for this chapter.

- How do these principles fit into your own spiritual aims and your meditation practice? Journal on your thoughts and insights.

Three Levels of Consciousness

THERE IS A LOT that we can realize and experience in meditation. We can feel relaxation and peace. We can contemplate spiritual principles to gain clarity and understanding. We can also use meditation as a creative time to review situations or memories, to heal and transform old hurts and regrets, to develop insights, and for problem-solving.

In this chapter, we will talk about how meditation allows us to experience the three levels of consciousness. You will find a picture depicting these levels in the book resources that I will reference throughout the chapter. These are fundamental awarenesses that each has its own quality, and implications for thoughts, feelings, and actions. This is an elevated practice of meditation, where moving from one level to another can deepen our experience and increase our capacity for concentration.

First is ordinary or body consciousness. I am female, my name is Anne, I live in Florida, I am writing a book on spirituality. These are all physical awarenesses. I am a human with a body in time and space. It is at this level where most of our thinking occurs, our emotional states, memories, etc. This is where we live our physical life as a human being. In the picture, this level is represented by the earth and space, the physical universe.

Second is the white area moving through the middle of the picture. This represents subtle or angelic consciousness, the realm of pure feelings. At this level, we are no longer directly aware of the physical world or ordinary thoughts and emotions; we are relating to deeper feelings, knowing, and a natural vibration of good wishes for all. In this subtle "region," we are beyond ordinary distinctions and ideas, and we allow our pure heart to lead. Here we can use the example of a baby. When we are with an infant, what happens to us? We become happy, curious, desiring to be close and interact. In that moment, we forget everything else, and we are in touch with our natural purity, our natural innocence.

So how do I use this in meditation?

In the subtle region, there is unlimited creativity and potential for healing and service. Each of our experiences will be unique, but I will give a few of my own examples. In meditation, I used to imagine that I was an angel with a beautiful, ethereal body of light and wings. I imagined God sending me on missions around the world to help people in different situations. At other times, I would imagine that I was only energy and I was next to God, radiating energy to all souls and to the world. In both of these, I felt a level of self-respect that only comes from elevated service.

We can also use the subtle region to bring up relationships or situations in a pure and protected emotional environment. In this way, we can see clearly and stimulate transformation at the level of our memory and emotions. I was able to use this method to heal painful memories from childhood and at work. I replayed a scene in my mind with the intention of healing myself, and then changed the memory so that my needs were met. I am rewriting the memory. The person now said or did exactly what I needed. The situation happened the way I needed to feel satisfied and good about myself. This is how meditation can help us heal the heart.

Finally, beyond the subtle or angelic level is the third level of consciousness. This is the soul world, or seed stage, represented by the golden-red light. This level is pure light. Here I am completely aware of myself, a point of light, silent, still, peaceful. In this stage, when I am still and silent, I can sense the presence of God. This is the level at which the soul can connect directly with God. We are vibrating at the same frequency, and so there can be the experience of a meeting. We can open our heart fully and communicate, share, even pray in the purest sense. This is one of the sweetest experiences that a soul can have. I will list two YouTube meditations below that will help stabilize in seed stage and have a direct experience with God.

What is the benefit of this stage?

This is where the soul is purified. Where the fullness of the self is experienced as well as direct contact with the Supreme Soul. This might be likened to eating the purest and most nutritious food for the soul. The intellect begins to awaken and become divine. The soul has touched Zero, and so its relationship to creation will never be the same. The soul's potential has been awakened at the level of pure consciousness.

This is the practice.

Points for Contemplation and Practice

- Look at the picture of the three levels of consciousness in the Book Resources. Write down the name of each level and write your own definitions based on your understanding of this chapter.

- In meditation, practice moving from body consciousness to angelic consciousness, and then into seed stage.

- Journal on your experiences and insights.

- Book Resources: YouTube Videos for Soul World/Seed Stage: Anthony Strano Link of Life Parts 1 and 2

- Guided Meditations: Pure Feelings and My Benevolent Nature

Bodiless Stage Part 1: Beyond Time

Bodiless stage is the soul's self-recognition beyond time, space, and matter.

IN THE LAST CHAPTER, we described the three levels of consciousness and how to practice the angelic stage and seed stage.

In the next three chapters, we will explore the soul world/seed-stage experience in more depth. Another name for this level of awareness and experience is "Bodiless Stage". The soul is experiencing beyond the awareness of the body, and beyond the ordinary functioning of the mind in time, space, and matter.

There is very little I can write about this. Instead, I will offer six techniques to help you create the experience for yourself.

Going up and beyond, through space, to the silent home

Sitting quietly with your eyes closed. Imaging a tiny point of light in the center of your forehead. This point is I, the soul. Once you are feeling calm, imagine the point floating out of the body and up, up, into the sky, into space, past the sun, moon, and stars, and gently settle in the soul world. A region of red/golden light. The home of stillness and peace.

Pulling your energy inward, becoming more silent and still

Sitting quietly with the body relaxed. Allow your awareness to be pulled inward toward your forehead. Become aware of each of your physical senses and gently detach them from the environment. Stop listening, seeing, and feeling the external environment. Bring all your attention to the mind, to your inner world. Make yourself silent and still, merging into that point of light in the center of the forehead.

Lost in a life experience

Choose an activity that you feel a natural resonance with. An activity where you naturally lose your awareness of your body and time. This may be music, art, exercise, or being in nature. Choose an activity where the "analytical" functioning of your mind is temporarily disabled. Then observe without analyzing. Notice how actions are being accomplished. Notice how you f eel.

Detached observer

Practice watching your mind, body, and behavior, in the moment, as if you are a completely different being. Watch in silence. Do not allow the mind to create language related to what the senses are bringing in. You may only be able to hold this awareness for a few seconds.

Age regression

Sitting quietly for meditation, start playing your life backwards on the screen of your mind. Slowly go back in age, giving yourself a chance to connect with the awareness, thoughts, and feelings of each age. When you reach younger than 5 years old, start going very slowly. We are moving beyond language here, so take your time. When you reach infancy, gently move into the womb. Stabilize there for a few moments, and then go to where you were before the womb.

Death experience *(remember, this is just an exercise)*

Sitting quietly for meditation. Create a scenario in your mind that would result in the destruction of your current body. Examples may include a car accident, a tornado, or a tidal wave. The idea is to allow the event to approach you slowly, in your mind. You are sitting in meditation, and the tornado is coming. Or you are in the car, in slow motion, heading toward the accident. In your mind, come to the conclusion that the body is going to be destroyed. Notice how you feel. Let the event keep coming closer and closer, paying attention to your thoughts and feelings throughout. Then let the event come through and destroy the body. The body is gone. Am I still here? Confirm this for yourself.

The whole idea of these exercises is to create an "in the moment" recognition that I am an incorporeal soul. Sometimes people ask me if this or that practice is spiritual. I am so tempted

to say, "Well, you are a spirit, so anything you do is spiritual."
But I don't say that. People are looking for steps and logic, and
I am happy to give that. However, the invitation of this book is
to go beyond logic into experience.

The leap to soul consciousness may sometimes seem so big,
and it is hard to imagine this awareness becoming natural. But
consider that soul consciousness is right next to you, like the air
in the room. All you need is to make yourself aware again and
again.

Points for Contemplation and Practice

- Using one or more of the suggested methods above,
  practice going beyond ordinary body and time
  consciousness, into the stillness of pure self-awareness.
  Practice distinguishing the self from the mind and
  from activities. The timeless self is distinct from
  everything contained in the realm of time and space.

- Journal on your insights and experiences.

Bodiless Stage Part 2: Sweet Silent Home

The kingdom of God (and souls) is within you.

I GREW UP HEARING stories of Jesus and what he said, and I remember Jesus saying, "The Kingdom of God is within you." Each soul has an innate pathway to connecting with God and the "Kingdom". In Raja Yoga knowledge and understanding, every soul is able to connect to God and the silent home of souls through the mind.

When we hear the word home, something in us already understands. Home is a feeling. It is an experience of comfort, belonging, love, and completeness. It is a sense of rightness, of being fully yourself and at peace.

These experiences live within the soul. They arise naturally when awareness becomes quiet and settled. When we speak about the Soul World as home, we are pointing to this inner awareness, an experience that feels familiar, even beyond words. In that awareness, God is present. There is a sense of connection, of being held, of everything being as it should be.

In the three levels of consciousness, we spoke briefly about the Soul World as the level where we are in seed stage, and we can naturally sense the presence of God. In this chapter, we will go further into the Soul World understanding and experience. We will explore this in two ways—through feeling (the heart) and through understanding (the intellect). Each offers a natural way to enter this awareness, and both lead to the same experience.

Let's start with the heart perspective.

There is a natural yearning in every heart to know where I come from and who I belong to. Think about people who are adopted. Many times, they feel as if something is missing, like they need to see and meet their birth parents to feel whole. The soul is not isolated, even though we talk so much about detaching and observing. In the heart, in the deep feelings, it is possible to feel pure connection and pure community. Looking gently here, maybe we can see why there is so much fear and sorrow in humanity. Souls do not know who they are, where they come from, or who they belong to. The Soul World experience fulfills this need in every human soul.

All souls come from this world of light. A dimension beyond time and space, beyond the physical universe. This is a world of stillness and silence, of perfection and peace. Safe, comfortable, home. This is the home of God and of souls. In the picture found in the book resources, we can see the Supreme Soul (God) at the top and all the other souls below, sparkling in peace. At this level, we are all together, connected, all of us belonging to one family. The Supreme Soul is the Father and Mother, giving containment, love, and nourishing energy to all souls.

Now moving to the intellect, the scientific mind.

The Soul World level of consciousness is where the soul is completely still. There is no movement of thoughts. Just pure awareness and pure feelings of self-recognition. This is seed stage. Nothing else exists but me in this awareness. However, I can open my awareness to perceive the existence of other souls at the vibrational level.

Looking at the picture, I can see the Supreme Soul (God) and all other souls, silent and suspended in this world of pure light. It is helpful at first to have a visualization for the mind to focus; however, this awareness of myself as still and silent is already within me. The ability to then be aware of others in this pure state is also already within me. I do not need to go anywhere or look for answers. In the silence, in the stillness of myself, are all the answers and the experience of pure connection that are also in alignment with natural law.

In this pure awareness, I can feel independent, like no one exists but me, and that is True. I can also be naturally aware of God and all souls beyond the consciousness of separation and distinction. The feeling is that we are all one, and this also is True. I am able to hold this dichotomy in my intellect, and I feel grateful to the Supreme Soul and this knowledge for enabling me to regain this mastery over the self and the world.

As you practice and play with these ideas and awarenesses, you will develop your own language that makes sense to you and stimulates the desired experience. This is not magic or ordinary imagination. You are using the mind and intellect creatively to experience your highest self-respect and also to fulfill the deepest needs of the heart. Welcome Home.

Points for Contemplation and Practice

- Guided Meditation: Sweet Silent Home

- Access the Book Resources for an image of the Soul World to contemplate. Sit with the image and try to have an experience as described in this chapter.

- Add this Soul World experience to your ongoing study and meditation practice.

Bodiless Stage Part 3: Pure Relationships

God helps us to heal our human heart.

As we continue on in this exploration of bodiless experience, we come now to relationships. Relationships are such an important and impactful part of our lives. They touch us deeply in the heart, and can be a source of great happiness and fulfillment, or confusion and pain. In Raja Yoga, we learn the method to fulfill the potential of all relationships, to fulfill the needs of the heart. For this, we need the Supreme Soul (God). Relationship with God offers a unique opportunity for the highest and deepest experiences of self-respect, sense of innate value, purpose, love in the heart, pure connection, and completeness.

Knowing who I am as a soul and knowing who God is, is necessary to experience a connection, a meeting, soul to Supreme Soul. God and souls are living consciousness, forms of energy—points of light—with no physical form, yet still unique beings with qualities. These distinctions are the same for both the soul and the Supreme Soul (God). Now we add the understanding that God is incorporeal, never takes a body, and therefore is not a human being. God is egoless, free from all vices, and beyond the direct experience of time and space. God is always pure, always in perfect self-awareness, fully mature, knowledgeful and wise, always present, and always generating benevolence for all.

When we come into connection with God in bodiless awareness, at the level of the soul, this relationship is naturally stable, clear, and unlimited. God is experienced as a pure mirror, one in which whatever we bring is met with truth, stability, and benevolence. In God's presence, the needs of the heart begin to be fulfilled naturally. There is a sense of ease, of being seen and known, of something within returning to its original state of wholeness.

You could say that God makes himself available for all relationships with you, or you could say that God's presence gives us the knowledge and power to realize the elements of relationship fulfillment within you. Whichever way feels right or makes sense to you, follow that. Let's look at the main relationships that we all have, and see how God's presence, how understanding who God is in relation to me, can help purify those relationships.

Father

God is my Divine Father—the one who gives me my identity. I am a soul, and my Father is the Supreme Soul. My connection to this Soul is unlimited and unbreakable. I carry the same spiritual DNA as God. I have all the same qualities: peace, love, purity, power, benevolence, bliss. As God gives to the world, so, as the child of God, I also give to the world. My Father gives me my inheritance of self-sovereignty, love, and peace.

Mother

God is my Divine Mother—the one who loves me, who gives me confidence and reassurance. As my Mother, God understands me fully and provides a beautiful, nurturing presence that allows me to grow and bloom into the best version of myself in the world. My Mother is patient and has faith in all the souls of the world. The Divine Mother gives comfort to the hearts of all souls.

Friend

God is my perfect Friend. The One who is always with me. Simply a thought away. The One who remains silently present, the comforting companion. God can provide me with the purest listening to my potential, as well as egoless, pure, and altruistic support through all situations. I can talk to Him freely and honestly, showing myself fully. And God accepts and loves me completely.

Teacher

God is the Supreme Teacher. He gives me knowledge, and encourages me to study and grow. He tells me the story of world history, past, present, and future. The story of myself and all of humanity. He teaches me about consciousness and matter, about love and my benevolent nature. This Teacher provides the knowledge to reset the identity of humanity and the pure consciousness of the world.

Guide

God is the True Guide. The One who lives in the unlimited and imperishable awareness of the Truth of consciousness, Natural Law, Spiritual Law, and awareness of the Time. This One, who is already in the most elevated stage, is coaching me toward that highest and purest stage for myself. God is available for moment-to-moment advice and guidance to keep me on track and moving forward. He will always hold the highest aim for me and shine the light of my perfection before me.

Child

God can also be my child. This subtle connection is about surrender and unconditional love. I exist to serve and support my love for God and God's purpose in the world. I am surrendered for service. Just as a parent attains meaning and purpose in life when they have a child, I have taken on this unbroken commitment of love for God and service to the world.

Explore each of these pure relationships on your own. Come up with your own definitions, your own language. Make each one meaningful and accessible to the heart. Use God's presence in meditation and fulfill yourself.

Points for Contemplation and Practice

- Guided Meditations: Safe with God, All Relationships with God,

- Book Resources: Link of Life 2/2

My Part of Service

My Benevolent Nature

My own benevolence is the discovery of a lifetime.

I WAS TEACHING A class with my husband last evening. He was sharing the importance of using your mind and feelings to generate positive energy toward people—all people, everyone. I had such a strong feeling at that moment to share my experience with the group.

"What Ken just said is absolutely correct," I told them. "I just want to share that I could not do it for a long time. For twelve years, I could not generate a pure good wish for anyone."

The reason for this was fear, hurt, and lack of self-respect. All of these were creating a storm inside my mind that took many years to calm down enough to use my mind to give. I told that class that my blessing for them is that it would not take them twelve years—that they will get it now. Then I gave them a method to bypass the storm of the mind, which I will share later in this chapter.

After fifteen years of meditation and service, I finally came to the realization that I, myself, am capable of giving. And also that whatever I am made of is worthy and valuable. This is the discovery of a lifetime, and my wish for all of you reading this is that you have your own similar realization.

So what does it mean to give with the mind, and what method did I share with the class?

First, let's review what we have already discovered about the mind. The mind is the soul's field of experience, full of thoughts, feelings, images, and memories. We have been practicing meditation daily, trying to experience calm, observe the mind, get to know myself, and heal.

When we start talking about benevolence, we may encounter a different level of difficulty. Although we may wish to be kind and generous in any moment, we may find this to be practically impossible. My emotions and reactions are too "loud," and I am not calm enough to naturally generate benevolence.

We then tend to look for an example to emulate—someone to inspire the possibilities of goodness in us. This could be the founders of religions, public speakers, historical or literary figures, or even people personally known to us through family or community. This looking for someone to emulate is a good practice, but it has only a superficial impact on my personality and internal world. It is better to find a way to access my *own* benevolence and directly experience this giving as something I am doing myself, from my own heart.

With all of that in mind, here is the method I shared with the class to access your own benevolence.

You may not be able to generate full-hearted love and good wishes for others at first, or on demand. But I am sure that periodically throughout the day, you do feel temporarily happy, or peaceful, or appreciative. There may be a moment where you notice the sunny day and have a wisp of happiness cross your heart. You may take a deep breath, one moment, and have a subtle awareness of the health of your body, and feel happy about that. Or you may meet a loved one and feel joy when you see them. These are moments we have every day. We don't have to try; they are spontaneous.

The method is to notice those moments and then immediately share that feeling with all souls in your mind, right then, in that moment.

For instance, let's say you feel happy seeing your child, spouse, or family member. In the moment you feel that feeling, notice it. Then create a powerful thought: *I wish that all souls feel happy in all their relationships.*

Or you may be taking a walk and feel a natural sense of connection with nature, of appreciation, of joy. Notice this and create the powerful thought: *I wish that every soul feels connected and happy in their body and with nature.*

So, what is the final understanding here? What matters most? It is that you already have the capacity to be benevolent, to give in a natural and authentic way. You don't have to try. Just invite yourself to notice your own pure feelings and then remember to give them to all, in the moment.

Just like any other habit, this one will take hold. And eventually, you will begin to recognize yourself as a good, pure, and benevolent being in this world.

The best part is that it all came from within you. This is the discovery of a lifetime.

Points for Contemplation and Practice

- Reflect on this chapter and make notes on your initial thoughts and feelings.

- What resistance is present? What hope?

- Let yourself fully express in your journal.

- If you are ready to try, start practicing the method outlined above and awaken your benevolent nature.

Elevated Karma

Inner awareness makes all the difference.

KARMA SIMPLY MEANS "ACTION," and action is a constant and natural reality in life. Even while sitting still, we think, we feel, we breathe. As long as I am alive, I am doing action. But when we dive into the law and philosophy of Karma, we find richness and power that is both confrontational and liberating.

In book one, we explored Karma on two levels. First, the idea of taking 100% responsibility for my life. Second is becoming aware of and taking responsibility for my feelings and reactions in real time. Both of these levels allow us to reclaim the power that we have been wasting in blaming and emotional indulgence.

In the *Spiritual American* podcast, the Karma lesson continued with level three, finishing Karma. At this level, we begin to notice the signs that old patterns have actually been resolved. These signs include a quiet mind on the subject and spontaneous change or resolution of related circumstances. We notice that we are no longer engaged with the issue in any way and that the situation itself often disappears. You get a new job, the person leaves, the illness heals, etc.

In this chapter, we will explore the fourth level, elevated Karma.

The main objective of this book is to open the possibility of living life with an inner landscape of soul-conscious benevolence. Consider the impact this inner awareness might have on the actions we perform. And by the way, it doesn't matter what actions we are doing. This is a *huge* shift and deserves a moment of acknowledgement. In spirituality, no action is better or worse than any other action. Consciousness is greater than action.

I am not talking about violence here, although that is included. Violence can be used to protect or stabilize a situation, as in self-defense. Consider that *all* action is actually neutral, and that it is the consciousness, or the living self, behind the action that makes the impact or feels the impact of the action. In the Ten Commandments, killing is forbidden. My understanding of the translation from the original text is that it is really "murder" that is forbidden. So what is the difference between killing and murder? The consciousness behind the action.

So now, the elevated potential. What would be the impact on my actions if I were in soul-conscious awareness with my benevolent nature activated? All actions—getting dressed, washing dishes, driving, speaking to someone, watching TV, walking, reading, bathing, eating, teaching meditation class, going to church. What would happen if I lived in soul-conscious awareness all the time?

This is the beginning of elevated Karma.

But we need two more aspects to make our actions and experience truly elevated. One is awareness of the Time or world situation, and the second is awareness of the presence of God.

These two topics have been explored in the introduction and in previous chapters. When we act in these awarenesses, we become a conduit for elevated knowledge and pure vibrations into the world—into the human collective consciousness, into the field of matter, into the subtle vibrational field of the elements of nature.

This is the essence of elevated Karma, the heart of spiritual service.

How do I begin this practice? I understand that I'm doing actions anyway. All actions have an impact on matter and on my own self-respect. So what would life be like, what would my self-respect be like, if I began to live in elevated spiritual awareness?

Each soul is sovereign and will have unique experiences and return of their Karma. All there is now is to maintain soul, time, and God awareness and see for yourself. The more you practice, the more you accumulate. This elevated spiritual inheritance is available to every human soul.

Points for Contemplation and Practice

- Review for yourself the basics of Karma law and philosophy as outlined in this chapter.

- Inner awareness for elevated Karma: Soul-consciousness/ Benevolent nature, Time, God.

- What is elevated Karma? Define this for yourself.

- Create a simple practice, try it, and then journal on your experiences.

Loving the World

Cooperation is caring from a place beyond sorrow.

Somewhere along the way, we learned to confuse worry with care. To fret over someone became proof of love. To carry their pain became a form of devotion. But worry is fear wearing the costume of love, and when you're weighed down by someone else's sorrow, what do you actually have to offer them? Your own heaviness. Your own constriction. You've joined them in the dark instead of holding a light at the doorway.

This brings us to an important principle: *Don't give sorrow. Don't take sorrow.*

The first part we understand easily enough—we don't want to cause pain.

But the second part runs against everything we were taught about compassion. We've been told that absorbing someone's anguish is empathy. That if we don't feel their suffering as our own, we must not really care. However, in spirituality, we have access to a much higher level of functioning with care, with love. We call this Cooperation.

Cooperation is the highest spiritual power. And we all have the capacity to be cooperative in the world.

So what is Cooperation? Let me explain the process.

Throughout our study so far, we have learned to discern our thoughts, to observe the mind with mercy and care. This is an act of love that creates the environment for what we may call healing, or the completion of sorrow. We are able to remember the past without pain. We are able to interact in the world with less emotional charge and less reactivity.

While emotional states are decreasing, something else is happening. We are saving spiritual *energy*. We are becoming more powerful. It is this spiritual power that gives us the ability to be stable, loving, and detached in any situation. This is called Cooperation.

Think of a time when someone you love was falling apart—upset, anxious, lost in their own storm—and you didn't fall apart with them. Maybe it was a child mid-tantrum, or a friend spiraling, or a family member drowning in worry. And instead of joining them in the emotional storm, you stayed calm, present. That doesn't mean cold or distant, just *stable*. You didn't stop caring. If anything, your caring became more useful. From that steadiness, you can offer a quality of presence that does not interfere with their experience. You are offering peace and stillness.

Consider how the sun works. It shines. It doesn't decide whether or not to shine on someone who's struggling. It doesn't dim itself in solidarity with those sitting in shadow. Its light and warmth are available because it remains what it is. You have a steadiness like that in you—a capacity to remain yourself in all situations and any emotional state, even in your own mind.

This is what it means to be cooperative, to be spiritually loving. Think about how a silent, still presence can feel to someone who is upset. Think about a time when you were very emotionally upset. What was the thing that you needed most? We have all had this experience, and also remember many times when others were not able to provide what was needed.

The thing I needed the most was a quiet, silent, caring presence so I could work through what I was feeling and get to the other side. Isn't that what I am doing for myself now? Aren't I learning to be silent and present so I can heal my emotions? I am learning to do, to be, exactly what I needed, what everyone needs. I am being loving and cooperative.

Take a moment now to consider this process of saving energy, reducing emotional intensity, and gaining the capacity to provide for others what they need to get well, to heal. This is Cooperation. This is love that actually helps.

So what should I do now?

I need to continue to watch my own mind and take responsibility for myself.

As I discern and transform, I become quieter, more still, even detached, while maintaining my loving heart. Then, gently, one day, try listening to someone else from this place of Cooperation. Listen to them and become silent inside. You still care, but you are no longer generating reactions internally. You are simply offering stability and peace.

You are becoming a blessing, an angel, an elevated presence in that moment. And this may be the only thing that can really help us in the end.

Points for Contemplation and Practice

- Reflect on the principle of "don't give sorrow, don't take sorrow".

- What does cooperation mean in the light of this principle?

- Consider how remaining calm and peaceful in all circumstances may be helpful to yourself and others.

- Try to change your approach in a situation where you would normally be emotional or reactive. Remain peaceful and generate soul-conscious awareness. Observe your experience and journal on your insights.

Spiritual Legacy

Serve the world and create your own destiny.

IT IS TOUCHING TO think about what our legacy would be. Not only what I leave behind, but what I am creating for the future. Children are a legacy. Whatever I put money and time into, like a career or starting a charitable organization, that is also a legacy.

So, what would constitute a spiritual legacy?

Once again, we are talking about things that are non-physical, matters of the heart, matters of self-respect. When reflecting on this idea of spiritual legacy, I found myself reviewing this Raja Yoga journey from the beginning. Writing this book series has been an effort to create a spiritual legacy by chronicling the journey in such a way that others can follow. Raja Yoga is a journey from pain, confusion, and corruption of self-respect to peace, power, and benevolence. It is a journey of awareness and pure self-recognition.

A student shared with me that he doesn't know where to begin. I told him that there is really only two practices:

meditation (the sitting-still discipline) and self-observation (the moving discipline). When we continually practice meditation and self-observation, we are creating the internal environment for healing and transformation back to the soul's original nature, to the "factory setting" of the self as a pure human being.

There are two other things we need to do in order to be fully successful. They are Study (which includes implementing knowledge into your practical life) and Service. We need to understand natural and spiritual laws in order to break free from old beliefs and conditionings that no longer work for us. And I need service to crystallize, for myself, my own pure identity. I need to make this whole journey about myself. We understand that I am not talking about ego here. I am talking about the presence of purity and goodness in the world. I am in the world, and I can make a difference by just being me.

When we start giving from the heart, when we are benevolent, that's when the spiritual legacy begins. Others are able to take for themselves, and we begin to experience the beauty of the law of Karma at the most subtle and personal level. I am receiving happiness, peace, and love while giving from the heart. And also, amazingly, I am getting *myself* reflected back to me as a good, benevolent soul who loves and serves the world. Just like God. Yes, just like God. This is not a small thing. In my opinion, this is the meaning of life. This is God's inheritance to us: the possibility of being like Him.

In the chapter on blessings, we discussed the power of remembrance and how, when others remember us, we receive energy, blessings that support and sustain us. As we feel our own pure, natural feelings and share them with the whole world, we are remembering the world, blessing the world. We are providing care and sustenance for the world, for all souls, and for nature. That is also what God is doing now. Being a source of love, care, and support for others at a time of need may be the highest action anyone can perform.

So what is the call? What is next? Continue to move from gross to subtle. From emotionally reactive to self-respect and benevolence. From being trapped in memories, pain, and fear, to being present in the light of Truth and Self-Realization. Every moment spent in this new awareness creates your future destiny and serves as a lighthouse for others to follow.

Points for Contemplation and Practice

- Reflect on your own Raja Yoga Journey through reading these books. Notice how far you have come. Give yourself honest and generous congratulations for being on this elevated journey.

- Write down two or three points that you feel are most important for you to work on moving forward.

- Reaffirm your love for yourself and the world. Take a moment to experience the self-respect of being a world-benefactor soul, alongside God Himself.

Continuing Your Journey

I F YOU'VE WORKED YOUR way through these three books, you have what you need to begin a serious spiritual practice. Everything is here, and you can return to it for the rest of your life and keep finding more.

But there is one thing these books cannot give you, and that's community.

A spiritual practice held entirely on your own eventually meets its limits. There comes a point where you want to sit in a room with people who are doing this work too, who are meditating and studying everyday, making internal effort, and engaging in service. People who understand what you are experiencing and who are surrendered in their hearts to the same world service you've been preparing yourself for.

That community exists. It's called the Brahma Kumaris.

So this is the invitation.

Find a Brahma Kumaris Center. There are more than forty Centers across the United States, in twenty states, with classes in many more places than that. If there isn't one near you, the website will point you to online classes, conferences, and retreats. The Brahma Kumaris go where they're needed, so distance is not really the obstacle it appears to be.

I'll be honest with you about what you'll find when you walk into a center. There's an aesthetic and a cultural inheritance that may, at first, feel like it's not for you. Most of the students at any given center in the United States are Indian, because the Brahma Kumaris are very well known in India and almost completely unknown here. They've been the best-kept secret of real spiritual practice in this country for decades.

What I want to tell you is this: by the time you've done the work in these three books, any cultural surface differences you encounter will not be a barrier. You have the knowledge. You have the experience. You have the confidence to look past the externals and recognize what's actually there—a community of souls who have given themselves to this path and to world service. They are your people, if you want them to be.

Learn more on the Brahma Kumaris US website:

Acknowledgements

T o my Beloved Father, Mother, Teacher, Guide, Friend... my Everything. To the One who, when I remember, I cannot create words from the depth of love and respect that I feel. My heart fills with happiness and gratitude, my eyes fill with tears of love and appreciation. You are the most Beautiful One, the Creator, the Beloved of all souls and of Nature. Your mark is on the heart and mind of each and every soul, and every soul will receive unique fulfillment from You at the accurate time.

To Brahma Baba, Mama, and all the Brahma Kumaris original jewels and senior Didis whose extraordinary faith and sacrifice continue to provide support for the world and spiritual sustenance for us all.

To the worldwide BK Family who bravely and tirelessly strive every day to purify the self and serve the world with love and powerful remembrance of One.

To my own family with love and gratitude. Whatever success I have is also yours.

About The Author

Anne O'Hare has been a lifelong student and spiritual aspirant. She has enjoyed a full life, including marriage, a child, and a satisfying career in Nursing, during which she earned a Doctor of Nursing Practice in Leadership. She has been a student and teacher in The Brahma Kumaris since 2011. This worldwide spiritual movement values purity, ongoing spiritual effort, and surrender for service. She has dedicated her life to serving the United States in particular, sharing the message of universal access to spiritual knowledge and soul-conscious experiences. Through Raja Yoga meditation practice and study, she encourages readers and podcast listeners to overcome the self-defeating forces within, courageously facing their mind to bring about healing, empowerment, and the emergence of their innate benevolent nature.

Connect with Dr. Anne: dr.anne.ohare@gmail.com

Listen to the Podcast: https://thespiritualamerican.com

HEAL · EMPOWER · SERVE

www.ingramcontent.com/pod-product-compliance
Lightning Source LLC
Chambersburg PA
CBHW021220130726
47988CB00002B/753